# Benedetto
# MARCELLO

(1686 – 1739)

Sonata for Treble (Alto) Recorder
and Basso continuo, Op. 2 No. 2
D minor / ré mineur / d-moll

Edited by
Manfredo Zimmermann

DOWANI International

# Preface

The music publishing company DOWANI is constantly expanding its library of music for the recorder. Manfredo Zimmermann, professor of recorder at the Wuppertal Musikhochschule and a specialist in early music, has edited and recorded this well-known sonata in D minor by Benedetto Marcello.

The CD begins with the concert version of each movement. After tuning your instrument (Track 1), the musical work can begin. Your first practice session should be in the slow tempo. If your stereo system is equipped with a balance control, you can, by turning the control, smoothly blend either the recorder or the harpsichord accompaniment into the foreground. The recorder, however, will always remain audible – even if very quietly – as a guide. In the middle position, both instruments can be heard at the same volume. If you do not have a balance control, you can listen to the solo instrument on one loudspeaker and to the harpsichord on the other. After you have studied the piece in the slow tempo, you can advance to the intermediate and original tempi. The continuo accompa-

niment can be heard at these tempi on both channels (without recorder) in stereo quality. All of the versions were recorded live. The names of the musicians are listed on the last page of this volume; further information can be found in the Internet at www.dowani.com.

As befits its origins, this music relies heavily on elements of improvisation, and we have included only the most essential embellishments and phrase marks. Players are invited to add trills, mordents, slurs and so forth at their own discretion. The same holds true, of course, for the realization of the figured bass (basso continuo or harpsichord), as can clearly be heard on the recording.

We wish you lots of fun playing from our *DOWANI 3 Tempi Play Along* editions and hope that your musicality and diligence will enable you to play the concert version as soon as possible. Our goal is to provide the essential conditions you need for effective practicing through motivation, enjoyment and fun.

Your DOWANI Team

# Avant-propos

Les éditions DOWANI sont toujours en train d'élargir le répertoire pour flûte à bec. Manfredo Zimmermann, professeur de flûte à bec au Conservatoire Supérieur de Wuppertal et spécialiste dans le domaine de la musique ancienne, a édité et enregistré cette sonate célèbre en ré mineur de Benedetto Marcello.

Le CD vous permettra d'entendre d'abord la version de concert de chaque mouvement. Après avoir accordé votre instrument (plage n° 1), vous pourrez commencer le travail musical. Le premier contact avec le morceau devrait se faire à un tempo lent. Si votre chaîne hi-fi dispose d'un réglage de balance, vous pouvez l'utiliser pour mettre au premier plan soit la flûte à bec, soit l'accompagnement au clavecin. La flûte à bec restera cependant toujours audible très doucement à l'arrière-plan. En équilibrant la balance, vous entendrez les deux instruments à volume égal. Si vous ne disposez pas de réglage de balance, vous entendrez l'instrument soliste sur un des haut-parleurs et le clavecin sur l'autre. Après avoir étudié le morceau à un tempo lent, vous pourrez ensuite travailler à un tempo modéré et au tempo original. Dans ces deux tempos vous entendrez l'accompagnement de la basse continue sur les deux canaux en stéréo (sans la partie de flûte à bec). Toutes les versions ont été enregistrées en direct. Vous trouverez les noms des artistes qui ont participé aux enregistrements sur la dernière page de cette édition ; pour obtenir plus de renseignements, veuillez consulter notre site Internet : www.dowani.com.

Cette musique repose à l'origine beaucoup sur des éléments d'improvisation ; c'est pourquoi nous n'avons ajouté que très peu d'ornements et de phrasés. Chaque musicien peut ou doit ajouter ses propres indications (trilles, mordants, liaisons etc.). Cela concerne également la réalisation de la basse chiffrée (basse continue ou clavecin) – comme on l'entend bien sur notre enregistrement.

Nous vous souhaitons beaucoup de plaisir à faire de la musique avec la collection *DOWANI 3 Tempi Play Along* et nous espérons que votre musicalité et votre application vous amèneront aussi rapidement que possible à la version de concert. Notre but est de vous offrir les bases nécessaires pour un travail efficace par la motivation et le plaisir.

Les Éditions DOWANI

# Vorwort

Der Musikverlag DOWANI erweitert sein Repertoire für Blockflöte ständig. Manfredo Zimmermann, Professor für Blockflöte an der Musikhochschule Wuppertal und Spezialist für Alte Musik, hat diese bekannte Sonate in d-moll von Benedetto Marcello herausgegeben und eingespielt.

Auf der CD hören Sie zuerst die Konzertversion eines jeden Satzes. Nach dem Stimmen Ihres Instrumentes (Track 1) kann die musikalische Arbeit beginnen. Ihr erster Übe-Kontakt mit dem Stück sollte im langsamen Tempo stattfinden. Wenn Ihre Stereoanlage über einen Balance-Regler verfügt, können Sie durch Drehen des Reglers entweder nur die Blockflöte oder die Cembalobegleitung stufenlos in den Vordergrund blenden. Die Blockflöte bleibt jedoch immer – wenn auch sehr leise – hörbar. In der Mittelposition erklingen beide Instrumente gleich laut. Falls Sie keinen Balance-Regler haben, hören Sie das Soloinstrument auf einem Lautsprecher, das Cembalo auf dem anderen. Nachdem Sie das Stück im langsamen Tempo einstudiert haben, können Sie danach im mittelschnellen und originalen Tempo musizieren. Die Basso continuo-Beglei-tung erklingt hierbei auf beiden Kanälen (ohne Blockflöte) in Stereo-Qualität. Alle eingespielten Versionen wurden live aufgenommen. Die Namen der Künstler finden Sie auf der letzten Seite dieser Ausgabe; ausführlichere Informationen können Sie im Internet unter www.dowani.com nachlesen.

Da diese Musik ihrem Ursprung entsprechend sehr stark auf improvisatorischen Elementen beruht, wurden nur die nötigsten Verzierungen und Phrasierungen hinzugefügt. Der Spieler oder die Spielerin darf/soll gerne eigene Ergänzungen (Triller, Mordente, Bindungen etc.) vornehmen. Dies gilt natürlich auch für die Ausführung des Generalbasses (Basso continuo oder Cembalo) – wie in der Aufnahme deutlich zu hören ist.

Wir wünschen Ihnen viel Spaß beim Musizieren mit den *DOWANI 3 Tempi Play Along*-Ausgaben und hoffen, dass Ihre Musikalität und Ihr Fleiß Sie möglichst bald bis zur Konzertversion führen werden. Unser Ziel ist es, Ihnen durch Motivation, Freude und Spaß die notwendigen Voraussetzungen für effektives Üben zu schaffen.

Ihr DOWANI Team

# Sonata

for Treble (Alto) Recorder and Basso continuo, Op. 2 No. 2
D minor / ré mineur / d-moll

B. Marcello (1686 – 1739)

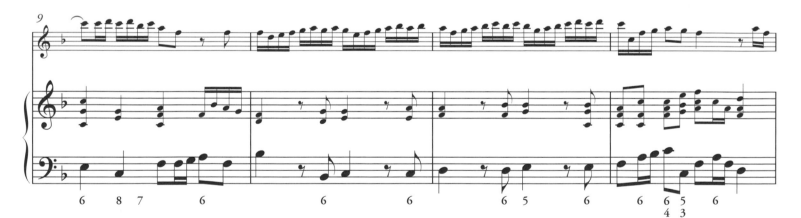

DOW 2504

# Benedetto MARCELLO

(1686 – 1739)

Sonata for Treble (Alto) Recorder
and Basso continuo, Op. 2 No. 2
D minor / ré mineur / d-moll

Treble (Alto) Recorder / Flûte à bec alto / Altblockflöte

DOWANI International

Recorder

# Sonata

for Treble (Alto) Recorder and Basso continuo, Op. 2 No. 2

D minor / ré mineur / d-moll

B. Marcello (1686 – 1739)

DOW 2504

III

Largo

4

# Benedetto
# MARCELLO

(1686 – 1739)

Sonata for Treble (Alto) Recorder
and Basso continuo, Op. 2 No. 2
D minor / ré mineur / d-moll

Treble (Alto) Recorder / Flûte à bec alto / Altblockflöte

DOWANI International

Recorder

# Sonata

for Treble (Alto) Recorder and Basso continuo, Op. 2 No. 2

D minor / ré mineur / d-moll

B. Marcello (1686 – 1739)

DOW 2504

3

4

# Benedetto
# MARCELLO

(1686 – 1739)

Sonata for Treble (Alto) Recorder
and Basso continuo, Op. 2 No. 2
D minor / ré mineur / d-moll

Basso continuo / Basse continue / Generalbass

DOWANI International

Basso continuo

# Sonata

for Treble (Alto) Recorder and Basso continuo, Op. 2 No. 2
D minor / ré mineur / d-moll

B. Marcello (1686 – 1739)

DOW 2504

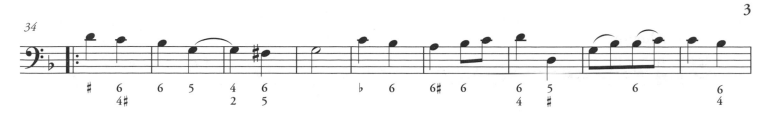

**Largo**

4

**Allegro**

**8**

9

Allegro

Allegro

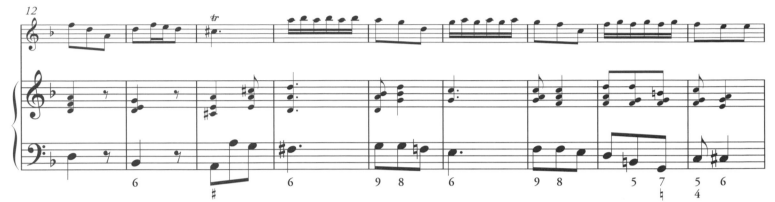

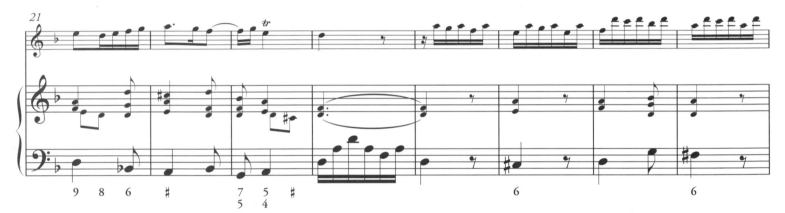

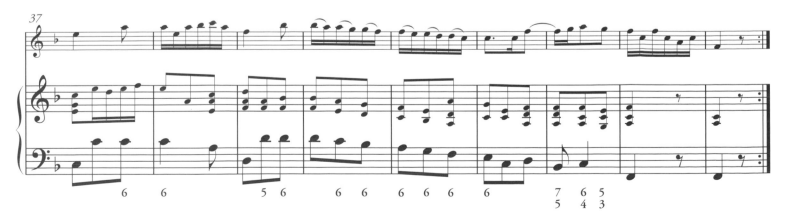

11

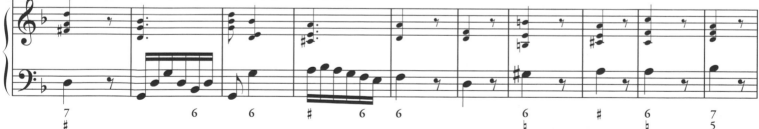

DOW 2504

## ENGLISH

DOWANI CD:
- Track nr. 1
- Track numbers in circles
- Track numbers in squares

[1] - tuning notes

⬤ - concert version

▢▢▢

- slow Play Along Tempo
- intermediate Play Along Tempo
- original Play Along Tempo

- Additional tracks for: longer movements or pieces
- **Concert version:** recorder with harpsichord i.e., basso continuo
- **Slow tempo:** the recorder can be faded in or out by means of the balance control / Channel 1: recorder solo / Channel 2: harpsichord accompaniment with recorder in the background / Middle position: both channels at the same volume
- **Intermediate tempo:** harpsichord only
- **Original tempo:** harpsichord only i.e., basso continuo

## FRANÇAIS

DOWANI CD:
- Plage N° 1
- N° de plage dans un cercle
- N° de plage dans un rectangle

[1] - diapason

⬤ - version de concert

▢▢▢

- Tempo lent play along
- Tempo moyen play along
- Tempo original play along

- Plages supplémentaires pour mouvements ou morceaux longs
- **Version de concert :** flûte à bec avec clavecin ou basse continue.
- **Tempo lent :** Vous pouvez choisir – en réglant la balance du lecteur CD – entre les versions avec ou sans flûte à bec. 1er canal : flûte à bec solo ; 2nd canal : accompagnement de clavecin avec flûte à bec en fond sonore ; au milieu : les deux canaux au même volume.
- **Tempo moyen :** seulement l'accompagnement de clavecin.
- **Tempo original :** seulement l'accompagnement de clavecin ou de basse continue.

## DEUTSCH

DOWANI CD:
- Track Nr. 1
- Trackangabe im Kreis
- Trackangabe im Rechteck

[1] - Stimmtöne

⬤ - Konzertversion

▢▢▢

- langsames Play Along Tempo
- mittleres Play Along Tempo
- originales Play Along Tempo

- Zusätzliche Tracks bei: längeren Sätzen oder Stücken
- **Konzertversion:** Blockflöte mit Cembalo bzw. Basso continuo
- **Langsames Tempo:** Blockflöte kann mittels Balance-Regler ein- und ausgeblendet werden. 1. Kanal: Blockflöte solo, 2. Kanal: Cembalobegleitung mit Blockflöte im Hintergrund, Mitte: Beide Kanäle in gleicher Lautstärke.
- **Mittleres Tempo:** nur Cembalo
- **Originaltempo:** nur Cembalo bzw. Basso continuo

**DOWANI - 3 Tempi Play Along is published by:**
DOWANI International Est.
Industriestrasse 24 / Postfach 156, FL-9487 Bendern,
Principality of Liechtenstein
Phone: ++423 370 11 15, Fax ++423 370 19 44
Email: info@dowani.com
**www.dowani.com**

**Recording & Digital Mastering:** Wachtmann Musikproduktion, Germany
**CD-Production:** MediaMotion, The Netherlands
**Music Notation:** Notensatz Thomas Metzinger, Germany
**Design:** Andreas Haselwanter, Austria
**Printed by:** Zrinski d.d., Croatia
**Made in** the Principality of Liechtenstein

**Concert Version**
Manfredo Zimmerman, Treble (Alto) Recorder
Mechthild Winter, Harpsichord
Steffen Hoffmann, Cello

**3 Tempi Accompaniment**
**Slow:**
Mechthild Winter, Harpsichord

**Intermediate:**
Mechthild Winter, Harpsichord

**Original:**
Mechthild Winter, Harpsichord
Steffen Hoffmann, Cello